HAUNTED HOUSE

VIRGINIA LOH-HAGAN

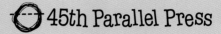
45th Parallel Press

Published in the United States of America by Cherry Lake Publishing
Ann Arbor, Michigan
www.cherrylakepublishing.com

Reading Adviser: Marla Conn, ReadAbility, Inc.
Book Designer: Felicia Macheske

Photos Credits: © Dmytro Vietrov/Shutterstock.com, cover, 1; © Jason Salmon/Shutterstock.com, 3, 11, 31; © xpixel/Shutterstock.com, 3, 11, 30; © Dan Kosmayer/Shutterstock.com, 3, 11, 31; © inhauscreative/iStock, 5; © Africa Studio/Shutterstock.com, 7; © forgiss/iStock, 9; © Marcel Jancovic/Shutterstock.com, 10; © Alex Veresovich/Shutterstock.com, 12; © Viacheslav Blizniuk/Shutterstock.com, 12, 17, 29, 31; © Pamela Moore/iStock, 14; © Elnur/Shutterstock.com, 15; © Salim October/Shutterstock.com, 19; © mevans/iStock, 20; © Alex Malikov/Shutterstock.com, 21; © aquariagirl1970/Shutterstock.com, 22; © sb-borg/iStock, 23; © TunedIn by Westend61/Shutterstock.com, 25; © Feel Photo Art/Shutterstock.com, 27; © kikujungboy/Shutterstock.com, 28; © wavebreakmedia/Shutterstock.com, back cover; © Dora Zett/Shutterstock.com, back cover

Graphic Elements: pashabo/Shutterstock.com, 6, back cover; axako/Shutterstock.com, 7; IreneArt/Shutterstock.com, 4, 8; bokasin/Shutterstock.com, 11, 19; Belausava Volha/Shutterstock.com, 12, 20; Nik Merkulov/Shutterstock.com, 13; © topform/Shutterstock.com, 15, 18, 19, back cover; Ya Tshey/Shutterstock.com, 16, 27; kubais/Shutterstock.com, 17; Sasha Nazim/Shutterstock.com, 15, 24; Ursa Major/Shutterstock.com, 23, 28; Infomages/Shutterstock.com, 26; © Art'nLera/Shutterstock.com, back cover

45th Parallel Press is an imprint of Cherry Lake Publishing.

Library of Congress Cataloging-in-Publication Data

Names: Loh-Hagan, Virginia, author.
Title: Haunted house / by Virginia Loh-Hagan.
Description: Ann Arbor, Mich. : Cherry Lake Publising, 2016. I Series: D.I.Y.
   make it happen I Includes bibliographical references and index.
Identifiers: LCCN 2015026834I ISBN 9781634704922 (hardcover) I ISBN
   9781634705523 (pdf) I ISBN 9781634706124 (pbk.) I ISBN 9781634706728
   (ebook)
Subjects: LCSH: Halloween decorations--Juvenile literature. I Haunted houses
   (Amusements)—Juvenile literature.
Classification: LCC TT900.H32 L65 2016 I DDC 745.594/1646--dc23
LC record available at http://lccn.loc.gov/2015026834

Cherry Lake Publishing would like to acknowledge the work of The Partnership for 21st Century Skills.
Please visit www.p21.org for more information.

Printed in the United States of America
Corporate Graphics Inc.

ABOUT THE AUTHOR

Dr. Virginia Loh-Hagan is an author, university professor, former classroom teacher, and curriculum designer. While she was writing this book, her television turned on by itself. A scary movie was playing. (It was spooky.) She lives in San Diego with her very tall husband and very naughty dogs. To learn more about her, visit www.virginialoh.com.

TABLE OF

CHAPTER ONE

WHAT DOES IT MEAN TO STAGE A HAUNTED HOUSE?

Do you love scaring people? Do you love having fun? Do you love Halloween? Then hosting a haunted house is the right project for you!

Haunted house designers scare people for fun. They use people's fear of the unknown. They make **staged** haunted houses. Staged means they're make-believe. These are different from real haunted houses. People believe ghosts live in haunted houses.

Staged haunted houses are a safe way for **guests** to get scared. Guests are people who visit your haunted house. Good haunted house designers make guests feel like they're in danger. But the guests aren't in any real danger. Haunted house designers make sure guests are safe.

Don't use sharp objects. Don't touch people. Create exits.

KNOW THE LINGO

Animatronics: robotic devices used to create humans or animals that look real

Apparition: a visual appearance of a person or thing

Camouflage scare: hiding a scary trick behind something that looks ordinary

Channeling: receiving messages from ghosts or spirits

Conjuring: using tricks to create paranormal effects

Hauntrepreneurs: haunted house designers

Haunts: haunted house attractions

Paranormal: strange things or happenings that can't be easily explained by science

Sensory assault: attacking all the senses by scaring people with sights, sounds, tastes, smells, and touch

Speaking in tongues: speaking a made up language

Throughput: moving as many people as possible through the haunted house

White noise: a hissing-like sound

Haunted houses are most popular during Halloween. But they can be fun all year long!

You'll have fun designing your own haunted house. You'll plan tricks. You'll create scary sights. You'll create scary sounds. You'll have guests touch scary things. You'll have guests smell gross things. You'll trick guests' senses.

You can also make some money. Professional haunted house designers charge $5 to $40 per guest. You can start by charging $5 per guest. You'll get better each time. More guests will come. You'll spend more. Then you can charge more. (Instead of charging, you can ask for **donations**. This is when guests give you money.)

Create tickets or wristbands for your paying guests.

41583

11137

6822694302 5

TICKET

6822694302 5

CHAPTER TWO

WHAT DO YOU NEED TO STAGE A HAUNTED HOUSE?

You need a place and time for your haunted house.

First, decide where you want to create your haunted house.

→ Consider places available to you. Some examples are your house, backyard, or school. You could also rent a space.

→ Make sure the space is dark. Turn off lights. Cover windows.

→ Make sure the space has an **entrance** and an **exit**. An entrance is a way in. An exit is a way out.

Second, decide a time.

➡ **Consider hosting at night. The darker, the better.**

➡ **Consider hosting over the weekend.**

➡ **Decide how many days or nights you want to host your haunted house.**

Third, create and send out invitations.

➡ **Make posters and flyers. Flyers are papers with event information.**

➡ **Use the Internet. Send invitations by e-mail.**

Get an adult to help you rent a space.

Consider your audience when thinking of a theme.

Think of a **theme**. A theme is a topic. The theme guides the event. It determines your decorations. It determines your tricks. Everything relates to your theme.

➡ Brainstorm a list of theme ideas. You have lots of choices. There's a monster theme. There's a graveyard theme. There's a prison theme. There's a hospital theme. (Think about things that scare you.)

➡ Choose your favorite idea.

➡ Write a story. Use the theme. Explain why the house is haunted. Record the story. Have it playing as guests come in. (Use a spooky voice when you tell the story.)

Staging a haunted house is like planning an event. It's also like directing a play. Making lists will help you organize. Check off things as you complete them.

➡ Collect things needed to create your **scene**. A scene is the setting. It's based on your theme. You'll need costumes. You'll need decorations. You'll need lights. You'll need **props**. Props are objects. They help guests believe in the performance.

➡ Make a list of the tricks and activities you want to host.

➡ Collect things needed for your tricks and activities. You'll find most things at a grocery store. For example, peeled grapes make great eyeballs. You probably have a lot of things in your house. Reuse whenever possible.

Pay attention to details.

TRY THIS!

Anything that glows in the dark is a little spooky. Greet your guests by creating a "glowing fountain." Place this at the beginning of the haunted house. Tonic water has quinine. Quinine is a chemical. It's what makes the water glow.

You'll need: bottle of tonic water (any size, room temperature), black light, roll of Mentos candy, notebook paper.

Steps

1. Remove the label from the bottle of tonic water.

2. Turn on the black light. (Don't get it wet.)

3. Roll a sheet of notebook paper around the top of the bottle. Make a tunnel for the candies.

4. Drop all the candies into the bottle at the same time. This makes a better fountain. The fountain sprays quickly. (Careful, this can be messy!)

You'll need help. Recruit some friends. Assign jobs to your friends. These are examples of some tasks:

Before people come:

➡ **Decorate the haunted house.**

➡ **Set up the activities and tricks.**

➡ **Apply makeup.**

➡ **Put on costumes.**

When guests come:

➡ **Greet guests at the door. Collect payment if you are charging.**

➡ **Guide guests through the haunted house.**

➡ **Scare your guests.**

➡ **Manage the activity stations.**

After guests leave:

➡ **Clean the area.**

➡ **Store everything nicely so you can reuse things.**

Consider hiring actors to perform in your haunted house.

CHAPTER THREE

HOW DO YOU SET UP A HAUNTED HOUSE?

Before guests arrive, organize your space. The key to a good haunted house is how it's set up.

➡ **Create a map. This will help you plan your space.**

➡ **Block off areas for several stations. Each station has a different activity or trick.**

➡ **Make room for a path. The path moves guests from station to station. It moves guests from entrance to exit.**

➡ **Make the path twist and turn. Most haunted houses look like mazes.**

➡ **Think of ways to "scare forward." Scare guests as they walk along the path. Scare them from the sides. Scare them from the back. This keeps people moving forward.**

TERROR BEHIND THE WALLS

Terror Behind the Walls is a company. It designs haunted house experiences. It's located in an old building. It was once a prison. It's in Philadelphia. The designers use special effects and lighting. They use digital sounds. They use robotic props. They hire more than 200 performers. Amy Hollaman is the show manager. She advises adding new things each year. She said, "Each year, Terror Behind the Walls gets a little bit better with new effects, new costumes, new makeup. We kick it up a notch. We raise the bar. We take it to the next level." For example, her team interacts with the audience. They pull people. They take people into dark halls. They put fake blood on people's faces. She also advises focusing on three things: scare, spectacle, and story. She said, "We want to have a balance between the things that scare people, impress and intrigue people, and bring them into the story."

Keep guests guessing about what's coming next.

Create a spooky setting. Make it hard for guests to see.

➡ **Replace lamps with colored lightbulbs.**

➡ **Put flashlights in various places. Give guests enough light to move.**

➡ **Use strobe lights to confuse people. Strobe lights give regular light flashes. It creates a slow-motion effect.**

➡ **Fill containers with warm water. Drop in glow sticks.**

➡ **Black lights make white things glow in the dark. Write scary things on walls. Write "Help!" Or draw blood splashes. Use white paint. Then flash the black light over it.**

➡ **Make fog. Buy a fog machine. Or buy dry ice. Drop it in warm water. (Buy dry ice right before your event. Have an adult help!)**

➡ **Fill spray bottles with water. Spray guests. This creates mists.**

Don't let guests see your friends' hiding spots.

Match stations to the theme.

Create terrifying experiences for your guests. Create stations. Have them touch and smell things. Blindfold them.

➡ **Create a smelling station. Have three bowls for guests to smell. Tell them it's dead body parts. (Use raw hamburger meat. Use kitty litter. Use nail polish remover.) Don't make smells too strong. You don't want guests to get sick.**

➡ **Create a touching station. Have them touch three different things. Tell them they're touching brains or other body parts. (Use wet noodles. Use pumpkin guts. Use peeled plums.) Give them towels to clean their hands.**

➡ **Record sounds for each station. One station can have the sound of a chainsaw. Another can have scratching noises.**

Prepare some activities and games. These can be stations. Match these to your theme. Here are some examples:

➡ **Put cold water in a tub. Put fake snakes in it. Put coins at the bottom. Tell guests to find a coin. While they're playing, have someone scare them from behind.**

➡ **Put dirt in a coffin-shaped box. Put fake bones in it. (Buy them at a pet store.) Have four guests play at a time. Have them collect as many bones as they can in a minute. The guest with the most bones wins. (Bury a rubber hand. Guests will be surprised to see the hand.)**

Keep guests busy with games and activities.

CHAPTER FOUR

HOW DO YOU RUN A HAUNTED HOUSE?

You've sent the invitations. You've set everything up. You're ready for the big night!

Greet your guests at the entrance. Guide them through your haunted house.

➡ **Have someone collect money or donations.**

➡ **Break your guests up into small groups.**

➡ **Take each group through your haunted house. Assign your friends to be guides.**

➡ **Start by telling them the story of your haunted house.**

➡ **Move each group through the stations.**

➡ **Wait for each group to be two stations ahead. Then move the next group along.**

➡ **Some guests may be waiting at the entrance. Prepare a quick activity for them. Set up a coloring or drawing station.**

Tell guests that they are entering at their own risk!

QUICK TIPS

- If you jump at people, they might hit you. Hitting is a possible reaction to fear.

- Use Jell-O.™ Mold it into the shape of brains or organs. Put it through a straw and make worms.

- Tear apart the heads and limbs of dolls. Put the pieces around the house. Put the chest in a jar. Put a glass jar over a head. Put a leg on the wall.

- Take black thread. Tape strands to the top of a hallway. Have several strands hang down. When guests walk through, it feels like spider webs.

- Make fake hands. Fill rubber gloves with sand.

- Turn cereal boxes into tombstones. Use fake names. Place by your entrance. (Don't write down living people's names. It's bad luck.)

- Make glowing eyes. Cut eye shapes in toilet paper rolls. Put glow sticks inside. Scatter them all around.

- Make extra money by selling drinks and snacks. Put fake spiders or bugs in ice cubes. Put them in people's drinks.

Guests will walk to each station. Give them enough time to do the task. Then move them along quickly. Focus on speed. Don't give guests time to figure out your tricks.

Create ways to surprise your guests as they walk through.

➡ Every once in a while, make loud noises. Scream for help. Scream in pain.

➡ Pick a moment to keep the house silent. Break the silence. Use air horns. Watch guests jump!

➡ Scare guests when they least expect it. Use a prop like a flying bat. Get them to look up. Then scare them.

➡ Quickly pop out to scare someone. And then disappear.

Keep your guests on their toes. "Distract and scare" is a popular haunted house strategy.

Use your friends. They can be "scare actors."

➡ Have them dress like ghosts or monsters. They hide in **scare pockets**. Scare pockets are hiding spots. They jump out. They scare people.

➡ Put fake blood on the floor. Have someone play a dead body. Then have them move.

➡ Have guests look at a mirror. Then have someone put a hand on the guest's shoulder.

When guests leave, remember to thank them for coming.

➡ **Ask guests to fill out feedback forms. Have them write what they liked about your haunted house.**

➡ **Get their contact information.**

➡ **Consider giving guests bags of treats.**

➡ **Tell them to come back next year!**

Thank all your friends for helping you create a successful haunted house.

THANK YOU!

D.I.Y. EXAMPLE!

STEPS	EXAMPLES
Where	My house.
When	Saturday night.
Fees	$5 donations.
Theme	"Dead Pirates."
Story	Sunken pirate ship haunted by evil pirate.
Lists	• Make a list of things you need. • Make a list of tasks. • Make a list of your stations and activities.
Create map	The path will be from the front door to the back door. Each station will look like a part of the ship.
Create scene	• Scatter glowing eyes all over the place. • Make fog with dry ice. • Make sounds of the pirate's peg leg. • Hang torn white sheets.

STEPS	EXAMPLES
Create stations	Blindfold guests. Give them three bowls. ◆ Bowl of pirate hands. (Fill gloves with sand. Add slimy water.) ◆ Bowl of pirate eyeballs. (Use large olives.) ◆ Bowl of pirate guts. (Put wet cooked noodles in cold water.)
Create tricks and scares	Create a station called "Dead Pirate Hunt." ◆ Have three friends pretend to be dead. ◆ Hide fake gold coins. ◆ Have guests look for the coins. ◆ Surprise guests by having the "dead pirates" grab them.

GLOSSARY

donations (doh-NAY-shunz) gifts of money

entrance (EN-truhns) the way into a room

exit (EG-zit) the way out of a room

flyers (FLYE-urz) announcements of events on pieces of paper

guests (GESTS) people who have been invited or pay to visit

props (PRAHPS) objects used to create a scene

scare actors (SKAIR AK-turz) people who perform in haunted houses

scare forward (SKAIR FOR-wurd) scare guests as they enter

scare pockets (SKAIR PAH-kits) hiding places

scene (SEEN) setting

staged (STAYJD) created, make-believe

stations (STAY-shunz) centers focused on a specific activity, idea, or trick

strobe (STROHB) light that flashes regularly

theme (THEEM) topic or subject

INDEX

LEARN MORE

BOOKS

Llimos Plomer, Anna. *Haunted House Adventure Crafts*. Berkeley Heights, NJ: Enslow Elementary, 2011.

Mitchell, Shawn. *How to Haunt Your House*. Pensacola, FL: Rabbit Hole Productions, 2009.

WEB SITES

Family Corner—Create Your Own Haunted House: www.familycorner.com/halloween-kids-family-2/create-your-own-haunted-house.html

Haunted House Association: www.hauntedhouseassociation.org

Kidzworld—How to Make a Haunted House: www.kidzworld.com/article/26135-how-to-make-a-haunted-house